Oxford
International
Primary

4

English
Workbook

Emma Danihel
Izabella Hearn

OXFORD

OXFORD
UNIVERSITY PRESS

Great Clarendon Street, Oxford, OX2 6DP, United Kingdom

Oxford University Press is a department of the University of Oxford. It furthers the University's objective of excellence in research, scholarship, and education by publishing worldwide. Oxford is a registered trade mark of Oxford University Press in the UK and in certain other countries

British Library Cataloguing in Publication Data
Data available

978-1-38-202009-1

10 9 8 7 6

Paper used in the production of this book is a natural, recyclable product made from wood grown in sustainable forests. The manufacturing process conforms to the environmental regulations of the country of origin.

Printed in China by Golden Cup

Acknowledgements

The publisher and authors would like to thank the following for permission to use photographs and other copyright material:

Cover: Artwork by Dan Gartman. **Photos: p3(a):** blickwinkel/Alamy Stock Photo; **p3(b):** Winchester College/In aid of Mary Seacole Memorial Statue Appeal/Mary Evans; **p3(c):** Marco Tomasini/ Shutterstock; **p16:** Rubens Abboud/Alamy Stock Photo; **p28:** Christopher Ewing/Shutterstock; **p29:** fox_workshop/Shutterstock; **p31:** Kir_Prime/Shutterstock; **p71:** Lorelyn Medina/Shutterstock.

Artwork by Dan Gartman, Mike Spoor, Kate Rochester, Chiara Pasqualotto, Chris Smedley, Francesca Marquez, Gustavo Mazali, Mark Beech, Maribel Lechuga, Oxford University Press, and Q2A Media Services Pvt. Ltd.

L.M. Montgomery: *Anne of Green Gables* (Puffin Books, 2014). "Anne of
Green Gables" and other indicia of "Anne" are trademarks and Canadian official marks of the Anne of Green Licensing Authority Inc. "L.M. Montgomery" is a trademark of Heirs of L.M. Montgomery Inc.

Every effort has been made to contact copyright holders of material reproduced in this book. Any omissions will be rectified in subsequent printings if notice is given to the publisher.

Contents

1 Life long ago

Anne of Green Gables

Read Anne's account to Marilla of the day her teacher tells the class he is leaving.

"I don't think I was crying because I was very **fond** of him," reflected Anne. "I just cried because all the others did. It was Ruby Gillis that started it. Ruby Gillis has always **declared** she hated Mr Phillips, but just as soon as he got up to make his **farewell** speech she burst into tears. Then all the girls began to cry, one after the other. I tried to hold out, Marilla. I tried to remember the time Mr Phillips made me sit with Gil – with a boy; and the time he spelled my name without an *e* on the blackboard; and how he said I was the worst dunce he ever saw at spelling; and all the times he had been so horrid; but somehow I couldn't, Marilla, and I just had to cry too."

From *Anne of Green Gables*, by L. M. Montgomery

A Tick the two sentences which are true.

Mr Phillips had made Anne sit with a boy in class. ☐

Anne thought Mr Phillips was kind sometimes. ☐

Mr Phillips thought Anne couldn't spell very well. ☐

Anne thought Mr Phillips' jokes were very funny. ☐

Mr Phillips spelled Anne's name correctly on the blackboard. ☐

B Answer these questions. Give evidence from the extract.

1 When does Ruby Gillis start crying?

_____

2 Why is it strange that Ruby Gillis starts to cry?

_____

3 Do you think Anne is really sad that Mr Phillips is leaving?
What does she say to make you believe this?

_____

C Find the word or phrase in the extract which matches the following meanings.

1 a talk you give when you are leaving somewhere

_____

to suddenly start crying very hard

_____

stop yourself from doing something

_____

_____

2 Find two words in the extract used instead of 'said'.

_____

_____

Verbs and adverbs

A Circle the adverbs in blue and the verbs in red.

lives   carefully   is   angrily   has   decides   happily

B Complete the sentences with a verb or an adverb from above.

Example: Anne skips to school _____happily_____.

1 She carries her bottle of milk _____.

2 Anne _____ at a farm called Green Gables.

3 Anne _____ red hair.

4 Her teacher _____ called Mr Phillips.

5 Anne _____ not to be friends with Gilbert because he was mean to her.

6 She speaks to him _____.

C Change the verbs into the past tense and the adjectives into adverbs to complete the paragraph.

In the classroom, Anne and the other children __silently__ (silent) sat and _____ (wait) for break. When the time _____ (come), they _____ (hungry) ate their lunch and then _____ (quick) returned to class. Only Ruby was late to lesson and when the teacher _____ (see) her arrive, he shouted _____ (furious) at her and waved his arms _____ (wild) in anger.

Adverbs

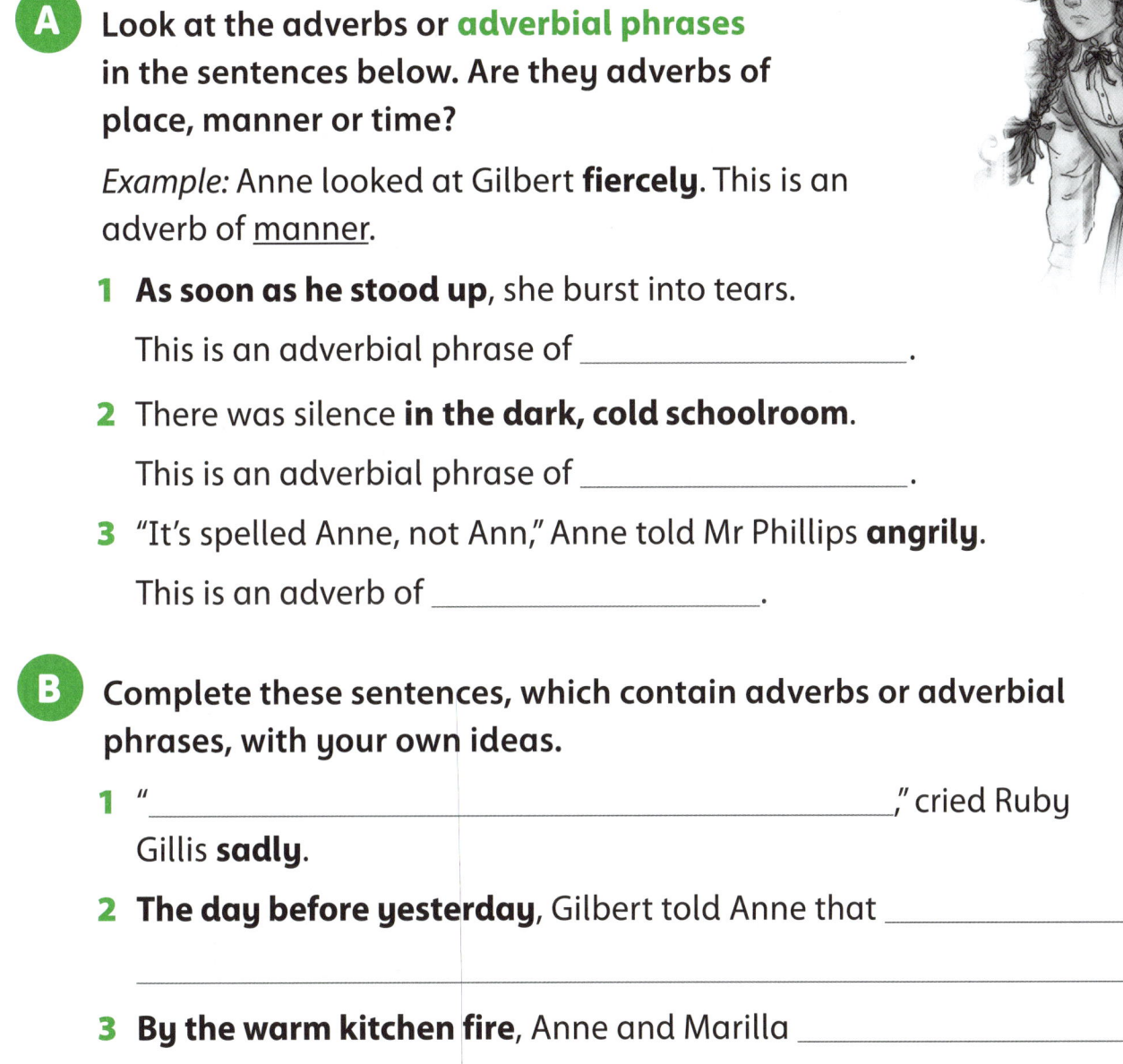

A Look at the adverbs or adverbial phrases in the sentences below. Are they adverbs of place, manner or time?

Example: Anne looked at Gilbert **fiercely**. This is an adverb of <u>manner</u>.

1 **As soon as he stood up**, she burst into tears.

This is an adverbial phrase of _____.

2 There was silence **in the dark, cold schoolroom**.

This is an adverbial phrase of _____.

3 "It's spelled Anne, not Ann," Anne told Mr Phillips **angrily**.

This is an adverb of _____.

B Complete these sentences, which contain adverbs or adverbial phrases, with your own ideas.

1 "_____," cried Ruby Gillis **sadly**.

2 **The day before yesterday**, Gilbert told Anne that _____

_____

3 **By the warm kitchen fire**, Anne and Marilla _____

C Add an adverb or adverbial phrase to complete the sentences.

1 _____, Mr Phillips made Anne sit next to Gilbert because she was talking too much.

2 The children packed up their bags and left the room _____.

3 Anne did her homework _____.

Vocabulary and adverbs

A **Circle the odd one out in each list of words below.**

Example: (well-behaved), geography, history, maths

1 happily, crossly, fond, horribly

2 abacus, chalk, schoolhouse, giggling

3 laugh, bucket, cry, shout

B **Explain why each of the words above was the odd one out.**

Example: Well-behaved is an adjective describing behaviour, whereas the other words are lesson subjects.

1 _____

2 _____

3 _____

C

1 **For each underlined section of the extract, circle one of the options. Then rewrite the extract using your options.**

Anne's teacher arrived <u>late / early</u>. The children were playing <u>quietly / noisily</u>. They were waiting <u>in the classroom / under a tree</u>. The teacher opened her bag <u>slowly / carefully</u>. Very <u>tenderly / gently</u>, she took out a small puppy. "We will choose a name for him after <u>class / lunch</u>."

_____

_____

_____

2 **What name would you choose for the puppy?**

_____

Clauses and commas

A **Underline the main clause in the following sentences.**

1 As soon as Mr Phillips stands up, she bursts into tears.

2 All the girls begin to cry, one after the other.

3 Four days ago, Anne spelled 'teacher' incorrectly.

B **Write three new sentences by adding different subordinate clauses to the main clause below. Use the correct punctuation.**

Gilbert pulls Anne's hair (main clause)

Example: All of a sudden, Gilbert pulls Anne's hair.

1 _____

_____

2 _____

_____

3 _____

_____

C **Finish these sentences by adding a main clause. Add a comma in the right place.**

Example: As it is raining, we stay in the classroom during morning break.

1 As it is raining _____

_____

2 As soon as the bell rings _____

_____

3 Thinking very carefully _____

_____

Irregular verbs, clauses and commas

A Change the verbs in brackets to the past tense and add them to the following sentences.

1 As it ____was____ (be) such a wet day Anne _____ (take) her umbrella when she _____ (go) to school.

2 Gilbert who _____ (be) a handsome boy _____ (go) to the same school as Anne.

3 As soon as the class _____ (have) their books on their desks the teacher _____ (be) ready to start the lesson.

4 On Sundays when there _____ (be) no school Anne and her friends _____ (go) to the river to have a picnic.

B The commas in the sentences above have all been left out. Read the sentences again and add in the commas. You might need to add more than one comma into some of the sentences.

C Write this main clause and this subordinate clause together in one complete sentence. Don't forget to add the correct punctuation.

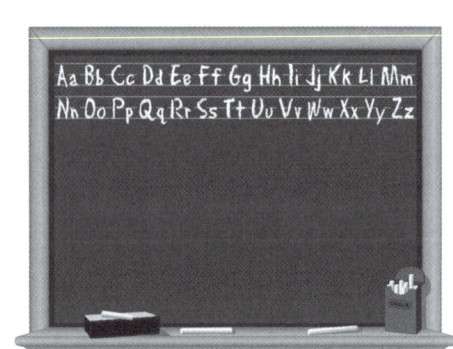

Mr Phillips wrote the alphabet on the blackboard (main clause)

who was the class teacher (subordinate clause)

_____

_____

Check my learning

Unit 1 Life long ago

Name _____

Date _____

☺ I understand and I can do this well.

😐 I understand, but I am not confident.

☹ I don't understand and this is difficult.

Learning objective	☺	😐	☹
Reading skills			
I can respond to questions about the text and retell events in my own words.			
I am learning to understand the meaning of a text, but also to think about what the writer might want me to think about it.			
Writing skills			
I can choose words to make my writing more descriptive and exciting.			
Language skills			
I can recognise and use adverbs.			
I can use commas to show meaning in sentences.			
I can recognise and use irregular verbs.			

I would like more help with _____

_____

_____

2 Beautiful bugs!

Features of non-chronological reports

 Read these sentences about fireflies.

Fireflies are nocturnal and produce a chemical that allows them to **glow** in the dark – each species of firefly flashes a unique light pattern.

They love warm, moist places so are mostly found in the humid areas of Asia and the Americas.

You might be surprised to know that fireflies are actually a kind of beetle.

It is thought that fireflies make light to attract **mates**, **defend** their **territory** or stop other animals eating them.

There are about 2,000 different firefly **species**. Most of them are a dullish, dark brown colour.

Fireflies live around wet or damp areas such as marshes, lakes or streams.

Writing a glossary

B Use a dictionary to create your own glossary.
Match the words in bold to their meanings below.

unique	nocturnal	humid	moist

1 _____ active at night time

2 _____ slightly wet

3 _____ warm and damp

4 _____ unlike any other

C Find two sentences from page 12 which, when grouped together, make a paragraph that answers each of the following questions. Make sure that you put the sentences in the correct order so that the text makes complete sense. The questions will be your subheadings.

What is a firefly?

You might be surprised to know that fireflies are actually a kind of beetle.

_____

_____

Where do you find fireflies?

_____

_____

_____

Why do fireflies light up?

_____

_____

_____

Alphabetical order

A Put the following groups of adverbs in alphabetical order.

Example: greedily, happily, hopelessly, hungrily, joyfully

1 warmly, zealously, quietly, oddly, vastly

2 cheerfully, coldly, curiously, casually, cleverly

3 softly, slowly, strictly, shyly, smoothly

4 rarely, regularly, rudely, really, roughly

B Put the following words in alphabetical order.

> scornfully   scarcely   scrupulously
> scrumptiously   scarily

C See how quickly you can use a dictionary to help you match the words in activity B to their correct definition below.

1 only just, almost not

2 wonderfully, deliciously

3 very carefully

4 frighteningly

5 doing something in a rude way

Punctuation

A Complete the definitions by using the words in the clouds.

to separate   full stop   strong feeling   a pause   the end

1 A full stop is used to mark _____ of a sentence.

2 A question mark takes the place of a _____ when the sentence is a question.

3 An exclamation mark is used to show _____.

4 A comma is used to mark _____ in a sentence or _____ a list.

B Add commas where necessary in the following sentences.

1 Insects have a head a thorax and an abdomen.

2 Although it was late they stayed to see the fireflies glowing.

3 If you want to live and thrive let the spider come alive!

4 Ants protect the queen defend the colony gather food and attack the enemy.

C Reorder the words to make clear sentences and add either a question mark or an exclamation mark at the end.

1 bugs and are pests Insects just _____

2 your in a wasp hair There's _____

3 He a tadpole caught _____

4 insect you an spot How can _____

Vocabulary, grammar and spelling

 A Complete the words by adding the missing letters and then match them to the correct pictures.

b_ _	_nt	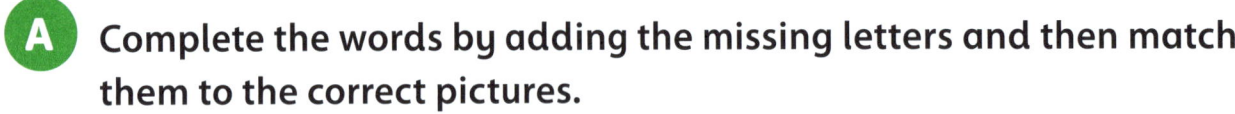
b_ _tle	sp_d_r	
w_sp	m_th	

B

1 Find and circle the **prefix** or **suffix** in the following words. Arrange the words in alphabetical order and place them in the correct columns.

dislike   (re)start   disadvantage   transform
childhood   goodness   anticlockwise

Prefixes	Suffixes
restart	

2 Now add two of your own words to each of the lists above.

C Choose one word from each box in activity B and use it in a sentence.

_____

_____

_____

Adverbs

A See how many adverbs you can find hidden in the grid below. There are 24 altogether. The first letter of each one is written below to help you.

b	r	i	s	k	l	y	e	s	t	e	r	d	a	y
e	a	s	i	l	y	o	u	t	h	f	u	l	l	y
a	n	g	r	i	l	y	n	o	i	s	i	l	y	e
u	r	g	e	n	t	l	y	d	e	e	p	l	y	l
t	r	u	l	y	m	i	s	e	r	a	b	l	y	e
i	n	s	t	a	n	t	l	y	e	a	r	l	y	g
f	a	i	r	l	y	h	u	n	g	r	i	l	y	a
u	s	e	f	u	l	l	y	e	v	e	n	l	y	n
l	a	z	i	l	y	h	a	p	p	i	l	y	l	t
l	o	u	d	l	y	g	r	e	e	d	i	l	y	l
y	e	x	a	c	t	l	y	c	r	o	s	s	l	y

angrily _____   h_____   b_____

i_____   b_____   l_____

c_____   l_____   d_____

m_____   e_____   n_____

e_____   t_____   e_____

u_____   e_____   u_____

f_____   y_____   g_____

y_____   h_____   y_____

Writing a non-chronological report

A Look at the paragraphs you wrote about fireflies on page 13. Answer these questions about common features of non-chronological reports.

1 What would be a good **title** for your report? _____

2 What type of sentences are the **subheadings**? _____

3 Is **formal language** used? Give an example. _____

_____

4 Are **adverbs** or **adverbial phrases** used? Give an example. _____

5 Are co-ordinating and subordinating **conjunctions** used to join ideas? Give an example. _____

B Now answer these questions about your report.

1 What tense is the report written in? _____

2 Which personal pronoun is used to make the report more informal and reader-friendly? _____

C Without looking at the report again, write a paragraph of three to four sentences about fireflies in your own words.

_____

_____

_____

_____

_____

_____

_____

Check my learning

Unit 2 Beautiful bugs!

Name _____

Date _____

☺ I understand and I can do this well.

☻ I understand, but I am not confident.

☹ I don't understand and this is difficult.

Learning objective	☺	☻	☹
Reading skills			
I can note key words and phrases to identify the main points in a non-fiction text.			
I can recognise the main features of a non-chronological report.			
Writing skills			
I understand how paragraphs and subheadings are used to organise ideas.			
I have practised writing a non-chronological report.			
Language skills			
I can recognise and use adverbs.			
I can put words into alphabetical order.			
I can add prefixes and suffixes to root words.			

I would like more help with _____

_____

_____

3 Tricks and truth

A playscript of *Aladdin*

Read this scene based on the traditional story of Aladdin.

Characters

Aladdin, a **carefree***, lazy boy, who never does anything to help his poor, widowed mother.*

Stranger, a mysterious old man.

SCENE 1

(In the street, where Aladdin is playing with his friends.)

Stranger	*(coming towards the boy)* Excuse me, young man. Are you the son of Mustapha, the **tailor**?
Aladdin	Yes … but he died ages ago.
Stranger	*(grabbing Aladdin's hand)* Oh dear, dear, boy! I am your uncle. I could tell straight away that you were my dear brother's son – you look so like him.
Aladdin	Really?
Stranger	*(happily)* Of course! Now, run along home and tell your mother I'm on my way to visit her.

A Answer these questions, using information from the playscript.

1 Which adjectives are used to describe Aladdin's character?

_____ and _____

2 Is Aladdin a good son to his mother?   yes   no

What evidence from the playscript supports your answer?

_____

3 What is Aladdin doing when the stranger meets him?

_____

4 Why is Aladdin surprised to be asked about his father?

_____

5 What does the stranger do when he finds out who Aladdin is?

_____

6 The stranger says he knows who Aladdin is. Explain how.

_____

7 Is 'happily' an adjective or an adverb? _____

B Using the playscript on page 20 to help you, write down five features of playscripts.

1 _____

2 _____

3 _____

4 _____

5 _____

Vocabulary

A Complete the words by adding the missing vowels.
Use the definitions below to help you if necessary.

_ct_r	pl_y	pr_p	_ _d_ _nc_
st_g_	th_ _ tr_	c_st_m_	

B Match the words from above to the correct definitions.

1 _____actor_____   a person who acts

2 _____   a place where a show or play takes place

3 _____   people who watch a show or play

4 _____   the building in which a play takes place

5 _____   clothing worn by an actor during a show or play

6 _____   a story for actors to perform

7 _____   an object used by an actor on stage

C Briefly describe the scene in this picture. Try to use exciting words.

_____

_____

_____

_____

_____

_____

Irregular verbs

A **Put a tick in the box next to the irregular verbs.**

(Remember, with irregular verbs, you can't just add 'ed' to put them in the past tense.)

ask	☐	sleep	☐	work	☐	pay	☐
read	✓	think	☐	say	☐	knock	☐
cough	☐	yell	☐	push	☐	run	☐

B **Put these irregular verbs into the correct form of the past tense.**

Aladdin ____ran____ (run) home and _____ (tell) his mother that he _____ (bring) interesting news.

Aladdin _____ (say) that his uncle _____ (see) him in the street and _____ (become) excited because he recognised who Aladdin _____. (be)

His mother _____ (speak) suspiciously and asked Aladdin if he _____ (think) the man really _____ (be) his uncle.

Aladdin replied that he _____ (know) that the man really _____ (be) his uncle and she would too when she _____ (meet) him.

So Aladdin's mother _____ (make) some delicious food which _____ (smell) beautiful.

When the uncle _____ (come), they all _____ (sit) down and _____ (eat) a wonderful meal.

C **Make sentences in the past tense using the following irregular verbs.**

hear	write	buy

_____

_____

Powerful verbs

A Separate the text inside the snake into eight **powerful verbs**.

noticedwhisperedclutchedleaptchargedclimbedcreptscreeched

_____ _____ _____ _____

_____ _____ _____ _____

B Replace the words in brackets with powerful verbs. Use the words above to help you.

Aladdin and his mother ____strolled____ (walked) up the hill and walked through the gate into the field. They _____ (saw) something behind the bushes.

"Oh no!" _____ (shouted) his mother, and _____ (held) Aladdin's hand.

"Shh, follow me," _____ (said) Aladdin.

They _____ (went) back to the edge of the field and _____ (went) over the fence. At that moment, a stranger _____ (ran) towards them.

C Imagine that the scene above will be performed in a play. Which role would you like? Give reasons.

_____

_____

_____

Powerful verbs and adverbs

A Put a tick in the box next to the powerful verbs.

boomed	☐	wandered	☐	looked	☐	dash	☐
surprised	☐	said	☐	glanced	☐	inform	☐
questioned	☐	walked	☐	gushed	☐	jumped	☐

B Use one of the powerful verbs above to fill each of the gaps.
Use the playscript on page 20 to help you.

1 A mysterious old man _____ over to Aladdin.

2 "Are you the son of Mustapha, the tailor?" _____ the stranger.

3 The question _____ Aladdin, because his father had died years before.

4 "Oh dear, dear, boy!" _____ the old man. "I am your uncle!"

5 "Now _____ off home and _____ your mother I'm on my way to visit her."

C Complete the playscript below by including a powerful adverb in the brackets to describe how the characters should speak.

Aladdin (___bellowing___) Mother, listen to me!

Mother (_____) What's wrong, Aladdin?

Aladdin (_____) My uncle is in town and he is coming here to visit us!

Mother (_____) Your uncle? Here?

Writing a playscript

A You are going to write scene 2 of the playscript *Aladdin*. Think of three questions to ask Aladdin to help you get started.

1 _____

2 _____

3 _____

B Complete the playscript below using your own ideas. Try to build up the excitement in the scene. Use the scene on page 20 and the text on page 23 to help you.

SCENE 2
(In Aladdin's home.)

Aladdin   *(rushing in, excitedly)* Mother! Great news! I just met my uncle in the street!

Aladdin's mother   *(suspiciously)* _____

_____

Aladdin   (_____) _____

_____

Aladdin's mother   (_____) _____

_____

_____   (_____) _____

_____

_____   (_____) _____

_____

_____   (_____) _____

_____

Check my learning

Unit 3 Tricks and truth

Name _____

Date _____

☺ I understand and I can do this well.

😐 I understand, but I am not confident.

☹ I don't understand and this is difficult.

Learning objective	☺	😐	☹
Reading skills			
I have practised reading playscripts, exploring how scenes are built up.			
I can respond to questions about the text and retell events in my own words.			
Writing skills			
I am able to choose and compare words, such as powerful verbs, to make my writing more descriptive and/or exciting.			
I can use alternatives for overused words like *said*.			
Language skills			
I can recognise and use adverbs.			
I can recognise and use irregular verbs in the past tense.			

I would like more help with _____

_____

_____

_____

4 Fantastic journeys

A fantasy story

A Read the following extract from a fantasy story. Add the missing apostrophes and speech marks.

Mitras picture was almost finished. She just needed a <u>pinch</u> of silver glitter to make it perfect. Mitra looked at Alisas picture and could see Alisa had used up all the glitter. Shed have to look in the classrooms store cupboard. There was bound to be some, somewhere, if she <u>rummaged</u> hard enough.

When Mitra entered the small room, she was surprised to see a door slightly <u>ajar</u> at the back of it.

Im sure that wasnt there before, Mitra said to herself. Curious, she <u>shuffled</u> over and pushed the door open.

How strange! Mitra exclaimed. She walked through the door and found herself in the middle of a pine forest. It was <u>coated</u> in thick, white snow and shone under the silvery moonlight.

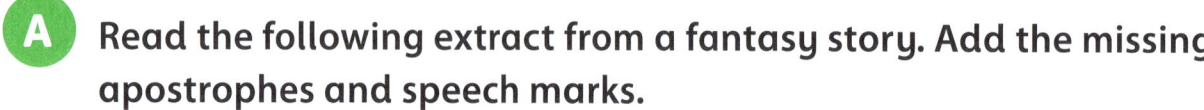

Mitra was <u>intrigued</u>. One minute she was in the classroom in daylight, the next in the middle of a wintry forest at night time!

I wish Id brought my coat! she whispered.

B Match the underlined words in the extract with a word or words with a similar meaning from below.

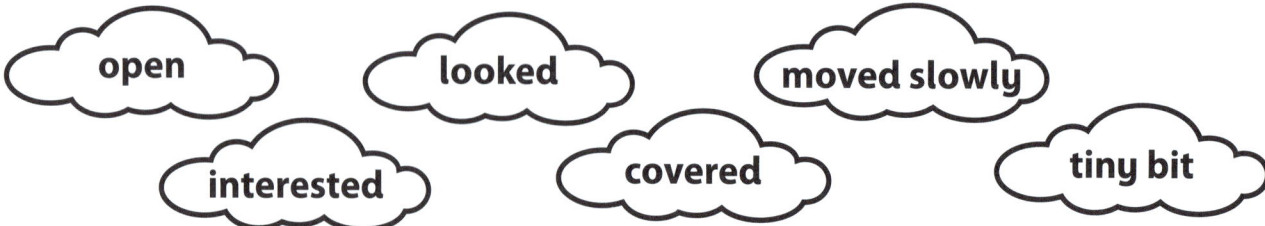

open   looked   moved slowly

interested   covered   tiny bit

C How do you know that this is a fantasy story?

_____

_____

Similes

A Choose the best adjective below to complete the **similes**.

> flat   dry   pure   sweet   sharp   quick   light   black

as ___quick___ as lightning   as _____ as snow

as _____ as honey   as _____ as a bone

as _____ as a pancake   as _____ as a feather

as _____ as a razor   as _____ as coal

B Complete these similes with your own ideas.

as busy as a _____   as free as a _____

as hungry as a _____   as slow as a _____

as strong as a _____   as quiet as a _____

C Match the simile on the left with its definition on the right.

as snug as a bug in a rug   very, very old indeed

as old as the hills   very safe and secure

as safe as houses   very comfortable and cosy

Speech marks

A Add the speech marks and punctuation to the sentences below.

1 What an amazing day squealed Alice

2 Would you like to visit me again asked the monster

3 I'm so tired exclaimed Sanjit

B Put the text in these three speech bubbles into sentences with speech marks. Can you think of alternative words to use instead of 'said', such as 'declared'?

Oh, this is so heavy!

_____

_____

_____

I am as fierce as a tiger!

_____

_____

_____

C Write a short piece of dialogue between the two characters. Remember to add speech marks and the correct punctuation.

_____

_____

_____

_____

_____

_____

Apostrophes

A Write the following contractions (shortened forms) in full.

aren't ___are not___   can't _____   didn't _____

won't _____   he'll _____   isn't _____

I'd _____   there's _____   we're _____

don't _____   that's _____   who'd _____

you've _____   they're _____   she'd _____

B In the sentences below, say whether each apostrophe is used for a contraction (shortened form) or to show possession.

Example: I **can't** find **Nina's** shoes. ___contraction___ ___possession___

1 **Who's** going to **Ali's** house after school? _____ _____

2 **What's** the new **girl's** name? _____ _____

3 **Eric's** kite flew away and **there's** no chance of getting it back.

_____ _____

4 **Lubna's** birthday is today and **they're** all gathered for her party.

_____ _____

C Add apostrophes to the sentences below where one is needed.

The boys are playing with Khaleeds art set.

Khaleeds paintings are of birds and animals in the jungle.

That girls sister plays in Jills rock band.

More fantasy fiction

Read this extract, which continues the fantasy story from page 28.

Mitra slowly walked further into the forest and further away from the cupboard door.

A quarter of an hour later, she was as cold as ice, so she turned around to <u>return</u> to the classroom. As quick as a flash, a squirrel jumped out in front of her. It was dressed as <u>grandly</u> as a king.

"<u>Halt</u>, spy of the snow queen!" he squeaked.

"Oh my, I've never seen a talking squirrel before. How sweet!" said Mitra with a smile.

"Sweet?" screamed the squirrel, as angry as a raging bull. "I'll show you who's sweet!"

"Captain Omerlon! Captain, stop!" came a <u>youthful</u> voice from the trees behind. "This is the human girl that the wise man <u>foresaw</u> would be sent to us. She will save us from the snow queen and free our people."

Then, through the trees, appeared a <u>handsome</u> young prince, with hair as golden as the sun. He was sitting on a unicorn, as white as snow, and surrounded by a small army of badgers, foxes and squirrels, running beside him on their two back legs.

Writing good character descriptions

A **Read the definition below.**

> **cliché**: an idea or description that has been used so often that it no longer has much meaning and is not interesting

Read the description of two main characters below.

> '… a handsome young prince, with hair as golden as the sun … sitting on a unicorn, as white as snow …'

> '… huge, round intelligent eyes as big as saucers … Their mouths are big and generous-looking.'

1 Which of the descriptions is clichéd? Explain your answer.

_____

2 Which description is more interesting? Why?

_____

3 Which figurative technique is used in both descriptions?

_____

B

1 Describe a clichéd hero/heroine from a book or film.

_____

2 Describe an unusual hero/heroine from a book or film.

_____

C **Describe your own hero/heroine. Use similes to help describe their character and appearance.**

_____

_____

_____

A Underline the six similes used in the story. Choose three of them and use them in your own sentences below.

1 _____

2 _____

3 _____

B Look at the underlined words in the extract. Match each word to a word or phrase below with a similar meaning.

good-looking _____

go back to _____

predicted _____

sounding young _____

stop _____

impressively _____

C Write four features of fantasy writing. Find an example of each in the story about Mitra.

Example: There are often fantastical beasts – the prince is sitting on a unicorn.

1 _____

2 _____

3 _____

4 _____

Check my learning

Unit 4 Fantastic journeys

Name _____

Date _____

☺ I understand and I can do this well.

😐 I understand, but I am not confident.

☹ I don't understand and this is difficult.

Learning objective	☺	😐	☹
Reading skills			
I understand how settings and characters are built up from details and I can identify key words and phrases.			
I can recognise the common features of a fantasy text.			
Writing skills			
I can recognise and use similes.			
I can use speech marks correctly and choose alternative words for 'said'.			
Language skills			
I can recognise and use apostrophes to show possession and contractions (shortened forms).			

I would like more help with _____

_____

_____

_____

5 Amazing animals

A newspaper report

A Complete the following newspaper report by adding a word or words from the list below. Use a dictionary to help you.

difference   overseas   aim   sit back   aware   extinct

Students in Ludhiana, India, have decided that they are not happy to _____ and watch the tiger become _____ in their lifetimes, so they have come up with their own <u>scheme</u> to save this beautiful beast.

They have created the wonderfully named 'Earn your stripes' <u>society</u>, with the one _____ of getting young people to work together to save tigers.

"Tigers are on the <u>edge</u> of extinction," says society member Nandan Kapur. "There is a need for everyone to be _____ of the importance of tigers."

He went on to explain that he wanted young people of the future to have the same chance as him to see tigers in their natural <u>habitats</u> and not locked away in zoos.

So far, the society has 1,723 members and its membership is growing every day. If you're interested in earning your stripes, you do not have to live in India to become a member. You can become an _____ member and receive regular <u>updates</u>.

It's an excellent <u>cause</u>, so why not join today? If we all work together, we can make a _____ to the future of tigers!

B Which of the underlined words in the newspaper report has a similar meaning to the words below?

purpose _____   near point _____

environments _____   plan _____

news _____   club _____

C Answer these questions about the newspaper report.

1 Who created the society?

_____

2 'Earn your stripes' means to prove yourself. Can you think of another reason the title of the report is *School Children Earn Their Stripes*?

_____

3 Do you think that this article was written for a student magazine or an adult newspaper? Explain your answer.

_____

_____

Adjectives – comparative and superlative

 A

1 **Put the adjectives in the brackets into either the comparative or the superlative form.**

Tigers are ___bigger___ (big) than cheetahs.

Blue whales are the _____ (big) animal on the Earth.

A giraffe is so tall that its legs are _____ (high) than most humans.

2 **Look at the adjectives in the brackets. Put them into the comparative or the superlative form by using 'more' or 'the most'.**

Dolphins are believed to be _____ (intelligent) than sharks.

Scientist believe that dolphins are _____ (intelligent) marine animals.

The tiger is _____ (endangered) than the cheetah.

Loss of natural habitat is _____ (dangerous) problem faced by the tiger.

B Write a paragraph comparing the two elephants using comparatives and superlatives. Look closely at the pictures and compare their size, weight and wrinkles.

Asian elephant	African elephant
 Up to 3.5 metres tall	 Up to 4 metres tall
3,000–6,000 kilos	4,000–7,500 kilos

_____

_____

_____

_____

Strong adjectives

A **Write out these lists of adjectives in order of intensity.**

1 good, wonderful, adequate

_____

2 weary, exhausted, sleepy

_____

3 pleased, overjoyed, happy

_____

B **Choose an appropriate strong adjective to complete these sentences.**

1 After playing football in the rain, Jade's kit wasn't just dirty, it was
_____ (horrible, filthy, unclean, awful, creased).

2 When Michael fell in the stream, his clothes weren't just wet, they
were _____ (drenched, soggy, moist, soaking, dripping).

3 The baby squirrel wasn't just small, it was _____ (little, minute,
tiny, slight).

4 When Andre broke a window, his dad wasn't just annoyed, he was
_____ (furious, cross, peeved, upset, angry).

C **Write sentences using strong adjectives based on the following ideas.**

1 You have been playing a team game. You are tired and hungry,
but happy that your team won.

_____

_____

2 You got caught in the rain on your way home from school and
you think your new trainers are ruined. Your mum will be cross.

_____

_____

Indirect speech

A Change the direct speech into indirect speech.

"What do you want to do when you leave school, Juan?" said the teacher.

"When I grow up, I'm going to be a racing car driver!" replied Juan.

_____

_____

_____

B Imagine two friends are having a conversation about what they are doing in the school holidays. Write the conversation they have. Don't forget to include speech marks.

"You won't believe what I'm doing in the holidays," said _____

"What are you doing?" said _____

_____

_____

_____

C Now change the conversation above into indirect speech and report what each friend said.

_____

_____

_____

_____

Verbs

A Complete the table below.

Verbs	Present (use he, she or it)	Present continuous	Past
save	he saves	he is saving	he saved
try			
stop			
grow			
increase			
see			
come			

B Choose the correct verb form to complete the sentences.

1 It _____ (takes/is taking) him 15 minutes to walk from home to school.

2 He _____ (is stopping/stops) his bike as soon as he _____ (is seeing/sees) the light go red.

3 The number of wolves in the wild _____ (is increasing/increases) in Canada now there are new protection laws.

C Change the passage below from the present to the past tense.

The students from Ludhiana help to make everyone aware of the decreasing population of tigers. They try to make people understand how important it is to act before it is too late. They want to see the number of wild tigers increase.

_____

_____

_____

_____

Writing a newspaper report

A Add speech marks in the correct places in the sentences below.

1 We need to act now to save tigers, said Nandan.

2 The girl shouted There is a tiger behind you! to the crowd of visitors.

3 At the end of the discussion, the child responded with I want to help stop the extinction of tigers.

B Write down three features of a newspaper report.

1 _____

2 _____

3 _____

C Using the information below, write a report about tigers. Include a made-up quote from Rajesh Kumar, the Tiger Conservation Society leader.

In an effort to increase India's tiger population, the Tiger Conservation Society has asked the government to create seven more tiger reserves. This would take the total number of reserves in the country to 49.

The number of tigers in India has gone up from 1,411 in 2006 to 1,706 in 2010.

The government will give financial help to people who are willing to move out of protected areas.

India has more than half of the world's population of tigers still living in the wild.

_____

_____

_____

_____

_____

Check my learning

Unit 5 Amazing animals

Name _____

Date _____

☺ I understand and I can do this well.

😐 I understand, but I am not confident.

☹ I don't understand and this is difficult.

Learning objective	☺	😐	☹
Reading skills			
I can recognise different types of non-fiction text and their main features.			
I can understand the main ideas of an account and respond to them.			
I understand how newspaper reports engage the reader.			
Writing skills			
I understand how the layout and presentation of writing helps to get across ideas.			
I have practised writing a newspaper report.			
Language skills			
I can recognise spelling patterns and work out the rules behind them.			
I understand how different adjectives can strengthen meaning.			

I would like more help with _____

_____

_____

6 Families of the world

A poem about family

A Read this poem.

My sister lives in Singapore,
Cousin Kate's in Cork,
My auntie lives in Ecuador,
Her nephew's in New York.
Madeline's in Manchester,
Michael's in Milan,
Winnie works in Winchester,
Joan lives in Japan.
The twins have moved to Tuscany,
Ronald lives in Rome,
Granny's gone to Germany –
And me? I live at home!

Catherine and Laurence Anholt

1 What title would you choose for the poem?

_____

2 Find the words in the poem which rhyme with the places below.

Singapore	Ecuador	Rome	_____
York	_____	Milan	_____
Manchester	_____	Tuscany	

B

1 **Match up the rhyming pairs of countries below.**

The Gambia	Bermuda
Barbuda	Uganda
Rwanda	Spain
Albania	Zambia
Ukraine	Romania

2 **Circle the word that does not rhyme in each list below. Then add another rhyming word to each list.**

Example: town, crown, ⦰tone,⦰ gown brown _____

  1 skate, place, space, chase _____

  2 village, finish, tillage, pillage _____

  3 roam, dome, home, helm _____

1 Order the lines of text and write out the chant.

Mum likes tea.

Gran adds milk

and sugar too.

I prefer chocolate.

What about

one two three!

Dad likes coffee,

One two, _____

_____

_____

_____ you?

2 In the columns below, write words that rhyme with 'two' or 'three'. Try to use the words from the chant above and add some of your own to the lists.

Two	Three
too	tea

3 Now write your own chant. Try to use the words from your lists.

_____

_____

_____

_____

Figurative language (alliteration)

A Underline all the examples of alliteration in the poem on page 44. Remember, alliteration is when the same letter or sound is repeated at the beginning of several words.

Example: 'sing a song of sixpence' or 'whisper words of wisdom'.

B Complete these sentences with a name that adds to the alliteration.

Example: <u>Marlon</u> moved to Mongolia.

Spain

_____ flew to Finland.

_____ immigrated to India.

_____ joined Joe in Jordan.

_____ happily hiked to Haiti.

_____ took a train to Thailand.

_____ biked between Bulgaria and Bucharest.

_____ sailed to sunny Spain.

C Use the names of your family or friends to make seven sentences of your own. Make sure they show amazing alliteration!

1 _____

2 _____

3 _____

4 _____

5 _____

6 _____

7 _____

Figurative language (simile and metaphor)

A Is the following statement a simile or a metaphor?

You are my sunshine! _____

B Think of a word to complete these similes and metaphors.

My best friend is as _____ as a rock.

Kim is as sweet as _____ .

I'm as busy as a _____ .

C Write a simile and a metaphor to describe yourself and the people you know. Use the examples to help you.

I am as brave as a lion and I'm so clever my brain is a computer.

_____
_____
_____
_____

My brother is always as hungry as a horse. His room is a disaster area!

_____
_____
_____
_____

Grandad is as old as the hills. He is a walking dictionary and helps me with my homework.

_____
_____
_____
_____

Figurative language techniques

A Add the missing vowels to complete the words below.

rhym_   _ll_t_r_t_ _n   m_t_ph_r   s_m_l_

B Say which figurative technique is used in each sentence below.

1 Ali ate an apple on an August afternoon.   technique: _____alliteration_____

2 She is a graceful gazelle.   technique: _____

3 He is as thin as a beanstalk.   technique: _____

4 There's a lizard in a blizzard.   technique: _____

5 Julia's head is spinning with ideas.   technique: _____

6 Atif slept like a log.   technique: _____

7 Ben barbecued Belinda's banana.   technique: _____

8 My brother is a bear with a sore head.   technique: _____

C Write an example of your own for each technique.

1 Simile: _____

2 Metaphor: _____

3 Alliteration: _____

4 Rhyme: _____

Writing a poem

A Read the poem on page 44 out loud. Make sure that you briefly pause at the commas and briefly stop at the full stops. Notice the rhythm of the poem. How many lines are there before each full stop? _____

B Using the exercises you completed in this unit, fill in the gaps below to make up your own poem about your friends and family. They can be silly sentences, but try to include rhyme and alliteration.

Example:

Katarina lives in Kathmandu,

My sister lives in a shoe.

_____ lives in _____,

_____ _____ in _____,

_____ lives in _____,

_____ _____ in _____.

_____ in _____,

_____ in _____,

_____ lives in _____

And me? I live _____.

Check my learning

Unit 6 Families of the world

Name _____

Date _____

🙂 I understand and I can do this well.

😐 I understand, but I am not confident.

🙁 I don't understand and this is difficult.

Learning objective	🙂	😐	🙁
Reading skills			
I can identify rhyming words.			
I have practised reading aloud with expression.			
Writing skills			
I can use a poem as a model for writing my own poem, copying the structures and technique			
Language skills			
I recognise and can use imagery and figurative language in poetry, including similes, metaphor and alliteration.			

I would like more help with _____

_____

_____

_____

_____

7 All together!

My Best Friend

Read this extract.

I first met my best friend at school seven years ago. My teacher had told me that there was to be a new girl called Belen and that I should look after her. She told me to go to the head teacher's office to collect Belen and bring her back to the classroom.

Walking through the school, I felt very excited. I started to think about the qualities I wanted my new friend to have. She would be <u>outgoing</u> and lots of fun. We were going to have such adventures together!

When I finally arrived at the office, the <u>awkward</u> girl waiting for me was nothing like I had imagined. She took one <u>timid</u> glance at me, and then quickly looked down at her feet again. She was small and skinny with a pale face that looked even paler and thinner because of her thick, straight, pale brown hair.

"Hello, Belen," I said <u>coldly</u>, not able to contain my disappointment.

"My name is Maria, not Belen. Belen is my second name," she replied <u>resentfully</u>.

"Huh, great start," I thought to myself. Without another word, I turned and started walking back to the classroom, with Maria following unhappily behind.

Seven years later, I can say that Maria is my best friend! We have had so many great times together. It just goes to show that first impressions can be wrong!

A Answer these questions about the extract.

1 Why is the narrator excited as she walks to the head teacher's office?

_____

2 What qualities does the narrator hope Maria will have?

_____

3 Why is the narrator disappointed when she meets Maria?

_____

4 Is the narrator wrong to be disappointed? How do you know?

_____

5 What mistake had the teacher made about the new girl?

_____

B Match an underlined word in the extract with the meaning below.
Use a dictionary to help you.

1 _____   in an unfriendly way, heartlessly

2 _____   loud, talkative, loving the attention of others

3 _____   embarrassed, not knowing what to do

4 _____   shy, no self-confidence

5 _____   doing something you don't want to do

C Read the extract again, then describe what Maria looks like.

_____

_____

_____

_____

Pronouns

A Underline the pronouns. Say whether they are personal or possessive pronouns.

Example: Dad adds paprika to <u>his</u> scrambled eggs and <u>they</u> taste yummy.   <u>possessive</u>   <u>personal</u>

1 My neighbour's garden is full of pretty flowers, unlike ours.   _____

2 Take my books and put them on the shelf over there.   _____

3 Ali dropped his brother's phone and cracked it.   _____

B Replace the nouns in bold with a pronoun.

1 Aimee gave **Aimee's** _____ textbook to **Aimee's** _____ friend Tariq so **Tariq** _____ could take it home and complete **Tariq's** _____ homework.

2 Pierre picked up the kitten and gently put **the kitten** _____ back in **the kitten's** _____ basket.

3 Omar and his friends agreed that **Omar and his friends** _____ would meet at the park after **Omar and his friends'** _____ lessons had finished.

4 My sister and I love going to **my sister and I's** _____ Granny's house because **my sister and I's Granny** _____ always bakes **my sister and I** _____ lots of sweet treats.

C Replace the nouns with the correct pronouns.

My brother Ali was looking after **Ali's and my** _____ neighbours' chickens while **the neighbours** _____ were away on **the neighbours'** _____ summer holiday. When Ali was feeding the chickens, he accidently left the cage door open and one of the chickens escaped. Ali ran around the garden trying to catch **the chicken** _____ until I came to help. Together, **Ali and I** managed to catch the chicken and put **the chicken** _____ back in the **chicken's** _____ cage.

Sentence types

A Look at the sentences below. For each one, write whether it is a question, an exclamation, a statement or an **order**.

Example: Stop talking now! <u>order</u>

1 Help! _____

2 It's nine o'clock. Go to bed! _____ and _____

3 What are you doing? I need your help. _____ and _____

4 Is that your painting? It's brilliant! _____ and _____

B Write the following sentences as an order, question, exclamation or statement. Add the correct punctuation.

Example: Tell the boy to sit down now. <u>Sit down, now!</u>

1 Ask Miyo what Kaito looks like.

_____

2 Tell the teacher how old you are.

_____

3 Tell the girl to stop making so much noise.

_____

4 You have dropped a heavy book on your toe. What do you say?

_____

C

1 Read the story *My Best Friend* on page 52 again. Write questions to ask Maria using the following words. Remember to use the correct punctuation.

What _____

Where _____

When _____

2 Add the correct punctuation at the end of each piece of dialogue:
a full stop, question mark or exclamation mark.

Come here, Ruby __	Where were you this morning __	That's unbelievable __
Yes, Granny __	I went fishing __	I'm sorry, Granny __

3 Now write your own short dialogue and include the four sentence types.
Write whether you have used a question, exclamation, statement or order.

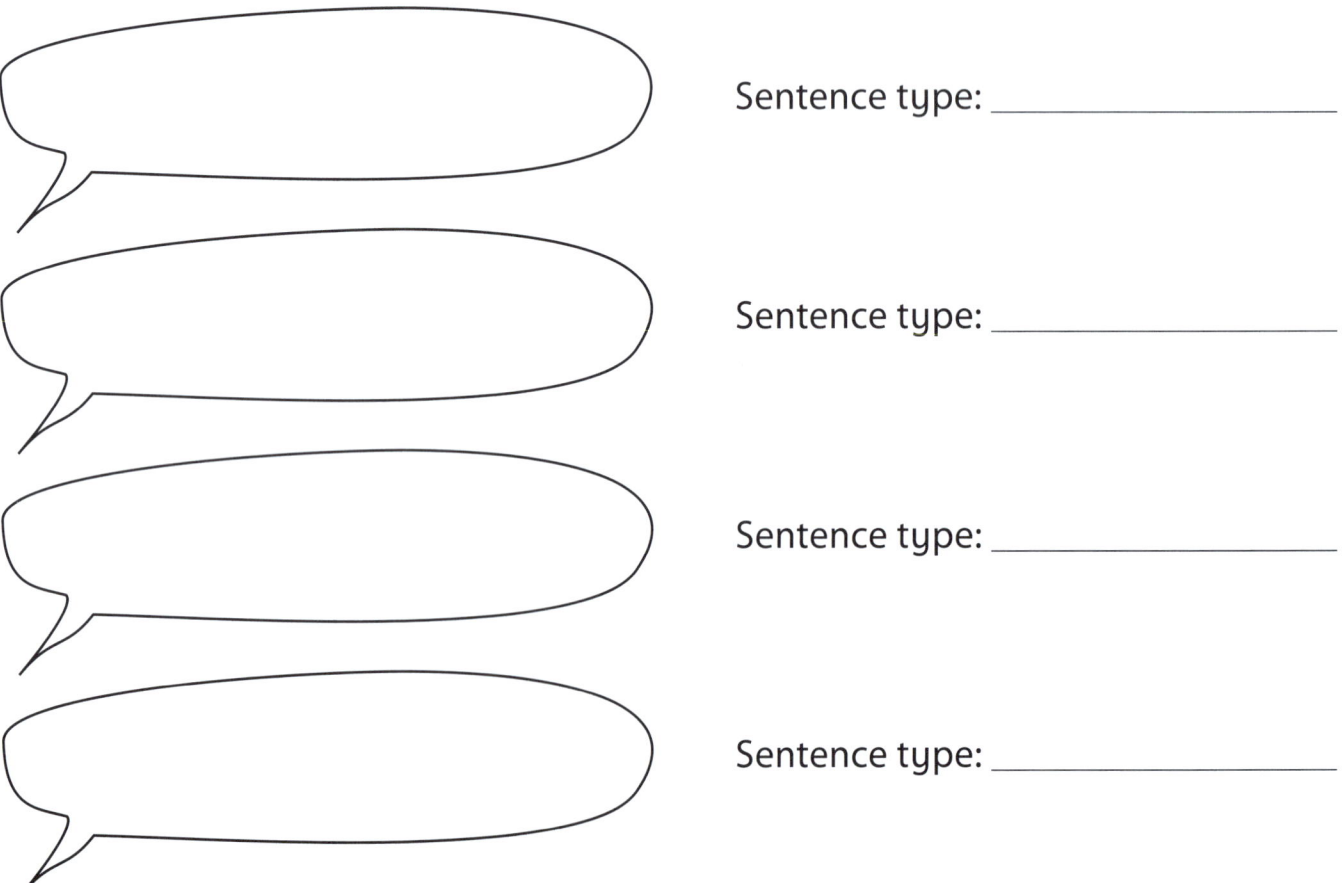

Sentence type: _____

Sentence type: _____

Sentence type: _____

Sentence type: _____

Homophones

A **Match a word from the left with its homophone on the right.**

new	won
saw	they're
through	too
their	fare
fair	weight
two	knew
wait	sore
one	threw

B **Fill the gaps with words from above to complete these sentences.**

1 Amy _____ the ball up in the air, and it went _____ the basketball ring.

2 I have _____ brothers and my best friend has _____ brothers _____.

3 The children are packing because _____ going to stay for a week at _____ granny's house.

4 Nobody in the class _____ the _____ boy.

5 I _____ Malek fall over and yell because he had a _____ knee.

Writing good character descriptions

1 List four things a good character description might include.

_____

_____

_____

_____

2 Tick the correct statement. Descriptive writing:

is always factual ☐

is always fiction ☐

can be a mixture of fact and fiction ☐

3 Descriptive writing can include similes and metaphors.   **true/false**

4 A good character description only describes what a person looks like.   **true/false**

B Write a detailed character description of someone in your family.

_____

_____

_____

_____

_____

_____

_____

_____

Check my learning

Unit 7 All together!

Name _____

Date _____

☺ I understand and I can do this well.

😐 I understand, but I am not confident.

☹ I don't understand and this is difficult.

Learning objective	☺	😐	☹
Reading skills			
I can respond to questions about the extract and retell events in my own words.			
I understand how characters are built up from details and am able to pick out the important words and phrases.			
I am learning to understand the meaning of a text, but also to think about what the writer might want me to think about it.			
Writing skills			
I can write a description of a person using detail to capture the reader's imagination.			
Language skills			
I can recognise and use possessive and personal pronouns.			
I can recognise homophones.			
I understand the grammar of different types of sentences.			
I recognise and can use a range of end-of-sentence punctuation correctly.			

I would like more help with _____

_____

_____

_____

8 World of water

Writing a persuasive text

A Read the beginning of this letter.

> Dear Mr Cable,
>
> I am writing to you **on behalf of** my primary school. We understand that a building company has **proposed** to build 20 new houses on marshland next to our village. We strongly suggest that you **reject** these **proposals**.

1 What is the purpose of the letter? _____

_____

2 What type of letter is it? _____

B Use these linking words and the facts below to add another paragraph to the letter.

Secondly   **Firstly**   **What is more**

• Great natural beauty and home to a lot of wildlife.

• Home to a dragonfly that is nearly extinct in this country.

• Not enough space in the school for 20 new families.

_____

_____

_____

C State your opinion again at the end of your letter. Start the concluding sentence: Start the sentence:

So, as you can see, _____

_____

Cohesive devices

A **Read the text about dragonflies on page 65.**

1 Find four examples of co-ordinating or subordinating conjunctions.

   a _____   **b** _____   **c** _____   **d** _____

2 Find one example of an adverb of time.   _____

B **Circle the adverbs of time.**

> therefore   firstly   next   because   then   later   after
> since   in addition   now   when   once   however
> although   while   finally   until

C **Add an adverb of time from activity B into each of the gaps below. (There might be more than one correct answer.)**

_____, the dragonflies mate. _____, the female lays her eggs on a leaf in a pond. _____, the eggs hatch and they become nymphs. The nymphs live in the pond _____ they develop into dragonflies. _____, the nymphs shed their skin to become dragonflies.

Prefixes, suffixes and roots

1 Use the correct prefix to make a word that matches the definition.

re-   dis-   mis-   un-

Word	Definition
_____re____ play	play again
_____ behave	behave badly
_____ known	not known
_____ agree	not agree

2 Use the correct suffix to make a word that matches the definition.

-er   -able   -ly   -or

Word	Definition
help _____	a person who helps
friend _____	a person who is kind and pleasant
conduct _____	a person who conducts
depend _____	someone you can depend on

B Circle the root of each of the words below. Then use a dictionary to find the meanings and use each of the words in a sentence of your own.

1 fearlessly

_____

2 unimaginable

_____

C

1 How many words can you make using the following prefixes: mis- dis-?

Examples: misbehave disagree _____

2 How many words can you make using the following suffixes: -able -en?

Examples: comfortable beaten _____

Changing root words

A Make as many words as you can by adding suffixes or prefixes to the following root words.

Examples: taste <u>tasteful, tasteless, distaste, aftertaste</u>

1 help _____

2 comfort _____

3 like _____

4 move _____

5 respect _____

B Complete the sentences by filling the gaps with a word that comes from the root word in brackets.

Example: Mum said that Dad's pasta sauce had a strange <u>aftertaste</u>. (taste)

1 I got rid of the old chairs because they were _____. (comfort)

2 My mum said I was being rude and _____. (respect)

3 I was surprised to hear they are twins because they are very _____ (like) each other.

4 Before she went to sleep, she _____ (move) her slippers.

C Use a dictionary to make three words from each of the following roots. The meaning of the root is in brackets.

bio (life)   tele (at a distance)

_____   _____

_____   _____

_____   _____

The water cycle

A Complete the following sentences. Use the explanatory text on page 128 of the Student Book to help you.

1 Heat comes from the __ __ __.

2 It causes water to __ __ __ __ __ __ __ __ __.

3 The water turns into __ __ __ __ __ __.

4 Water vapour forms __ __ __ __ __ __.

5 __ __ __ __ carries clouds over the land.

6 Water falls as __ __ __ __.

7 Rain runs off into __ __ __ __ __ __.

8 It soaks through the __ __ __ __.

9 The __ __ __ __ __ is called groundwater.

10 The water evaporates and the __ __ __ __ __ begins again.

B Can you find the ten words from above in the word search below?

A	E	C	Y	C	L	E	W	B	D
B	F	L	S	L	A	E	A	G	I
E	V	A	P	O	R	A	T	E	H
C	A	M	T	U	C	F	E	N	S
D	P	N	U	D	J	O	R	U	O
G	O	O	V	S	U	N	K	P	I
H	U	P	W	Y	Q	W	V	L	L
I	R	A	I	N	W	R	I	Z	M
J	Q	R	X	Z	A	X	S	N	Y
K	S	T	R	E	A	M	S	T	D

Writing an explanatory text

Read the text below about dragonflies.

A dragonfly has a <u>lifespan</u> of more than one year, but very little of it is actually spent as an adult dragonfly. There are three stages in a dragonfly's life cycle: the egg, the nymph and the adult dragonfly.

A male and female dragonfly will mate while they are flying in the air. Afterwards, the female dragonfly will lay her eggs on a plant leaf in the water. The life cycle has begun.

The dragonfly eggs <u>hatch</u> into <u>nymphs</u>. Dragonfly nymphs live in the water while they grow and change into dragonflies. This can take up to four years. Dragonfly nymphs live in ponds because the water is calmer than in streams or rivers.

In springtime, once the nymph is fully grown, it will crawl out of the water up the <u>stem</u> of a plant. The nymph will <u>shed</u> its skin on to the stem of the plant and will then be an adult dragonfly. The adult dragonfly will look for a <u>mate</u> and the whole cycle begins again. Adult dragonflies live for about two months.

A Make a glossary by matching the underlined words in the extract to the definitions below.

1 _____   the length of a whole lifetime

2 _____   the part of a plant that supports the leaves

3 _____   young dragonflies

4 _____   to break out of an egg

5 _____   take off, remove

6 _____   a partner of the opposite sex

B Which subheading would be best for each paragraph?

The nymph stage   The life cycle of a dragonfly

The egg stage   The adult dragonfly

1 _____

2 _____

3 _____

4 _____

C Find out about another animal that lives in or near water. Then use the information to write a short explanatory text. Remember to use formal language and organise your text into paragraphs with subheadings.

_____

_____

_____

_____

_____

_____

_____

_____

_____

_____

_____

_____

_____

_____

_____

Check my learning

Unit 8 World of water

Name _____

Date _____

☺ I understand and I can do this well.

😐 I understand, but I am not confident.

☹ I don't understand and this is difficult.

Learning objective	☺	😐	☹
Reading skills			
I can recognise different types of non-fiction text and their main features.			
I understand how persuasive writing is used to convince a reader.			
I understand how paragraphs are used to organise ideas.			
Writing skills			
I can present a point of view in ordered points.			
I can show awareness of the reader by writing in an appropriate style.			
Language skills			
I understand the use of co-ordinating or subordinating conjunctions and adverbs of time to structure an argument.			
I recognise and can use prefixes and suffixes.			
I recognise and can use words with common roots.			

I would like more help with _____

_____

_____

9 Poems for all seasons

A poem about changing seasons

THE TREE AND THE POOL

"I don't want my leaves to drop," said the tree.
"I don't want to <u>freeze</u>," said the pool.
"I don't want to smile," said the <u>sombre</u> man,
"Or ever to cry," said the <u>Fool</u>.

"I don't want to open," said the <u>bud</u>,
"I don't want to end," said the night.
"I don't want to rise," said the neap-tide, *
"Or ever to fall," said the kite.

They wished and they <u>murmured</u> and whispered,
They said that to change was a crime,
Then a voice from nowhere answered.
"You must do what I say," said Time.

Brian Patten

* A neap-tide comes twice a month, in the first and third quarters of the moon.

A Look at the underlined words in the poem and match them to their meaning below.

1 _____   spoke quietly or unclearly

2 _____   serious or gloomy

3 _____   the part of a plant that develops
                                     into a leaf or a flower

4 _____   a clown or someone who tells jokes

5 _____   when water turns to ice

B The poet has used different imagery to make the reader think about the weather and changing seasons. Find references to the following:

autumn _____

_____

winter _____

_____

spring _____

_____

a windy day _____

_____

C Write down three things that are the same in the first verse and the second verse.

1 _____

2 _____

3 _____

Spellings and sounds

A For each list below, underline the part of the word that has the same letters. Then circle the word in which these letters are pronounced differently.

Example: <u>fow</u>l (<u>bowl</u>) <u>tow</u>el <u>ow</u>l

1 loud   shout   pour   round

2 dear   beard   fear   learn

3 although   cough   though   dough

4 love   move   above   gloves

5 eight   weight   height   neighbour

6 oar   oat   coach   soak

7 jewel   blew   sew   knew

8 dice   notice   slice   iceberg

9 shall   all   hallway   wall

10 caught   naughty   daughter   laughter

B Underline the word which rhymes with the examples given.

fair   tear (water coming from your eye)
             <u>tear (to rip something)</u>

so   bow (to bend your knee or body)
             bow (a decorative ribbon)

froze   close (shut the door)
             close (not far away)

seed   lead (a heavy metal)
             lead (to show someone the way)

C **Write the two different meanings of the words below, which are spelled the same but pronounced differently.**

row   1. An argument. 2. A line of people or things. _____

wind _____

excuse _____

minute _____

present _____

Syllables

A Divide these five words into syllables and then write them in the correct column, as shown in the example.

happy   children   allergy   campfire   horribly   butterfly

Two syllables	Three syllables
hap / py	

B Match the syllables to make complete words and write them in the correct column to show the number of syllables each complete word contains.

sum	on	er
drag	mer	fly
lim	heart	ick
win	ter	ed
kind	er	

Two syllables	Three syllables
sum / mer	

C Write the name of a friend or relative in each column according to the number of syllables in their name.

One syllable	Two syllables	Three syllables	Four syllables
Bill	Greta	Damian	Izabella
_____	_____	_____	_____

Season's poem

A Read the text in the boxes and match them to the correct verse of the poem. Write the words on the lines.

falling leaves
and stormy seas.

buzzing bees,
a warming breeze.

Sunny days
An early haze,

_____

_____

Autumn gold
the winds are cold,

_____

_____

colours, blossom,
fragile, awesome!

mountains glow
with fresh white snow.

Winter's bare
with crisp fresh air

_____

_____

Spring brings flowers,
gentle showers,

_____

_____

B Find and write down the words from the poem that rhyme with 'please'. Then add two more words of your own.

_____

_____

C Look at the pictures and read the poem slowly. Then cover the words and see if you can remember the poem.

Writing a poem

A Look again at the poem on page 68. Write some similar sentences using the clues in brackets below.

Example: (summer) "I don't want <u>to dry up</u>," said the puddle.

(autumn) "We don't want _____," said the flowers.

(winter) "I don't want _____," said the river.

(morning) "We don't want _____," said the stars.

(sunset) "I don't want _____," said the sun.

(winter) "I don't want _____," said the snowman.

B Now write a poem of your own. Use the correct punctuation and try to find two nouns that rhyme for lines 2 and 4.

Example: "I don't want to wake," said the bear. (Line 2)
"I don't want to sleep," said the hare. (Line 4)

"I don't want _____," said the _____

"I don't want _____," said the _____

"I don't want _____," said the _____

"Or _____," said the _____

Check my learning

Unit 9 Poems for all seasons

Name _____

Date _____

☺ I understand and I can do this well.

😐 I understand, but I am not confident.

☹ I don't understand and this is difficult.

Learning objective	☺	😐	☹
Reading skills			
I have explored imagery and figurative language in poems.			
I can apply what I already know to help me read unfamiliar words.			
Writing skills			
I can use expressive and descriptive language to make a certain mood in a poem.			
I can write a poem with a strong rhythm and the same number of syllables in each line.			
Language skills			
I can spell words with common letter strings but different pronunciations.			

I would like more help with _____

_____

_____

_____

Writing and vocabulary

How to make a king's tower

The pictures below show how to make a king's tower.

A Add numbers 1–6 to the pictures, to show the correct order in which to make the king's tower. The first one has been done for you.

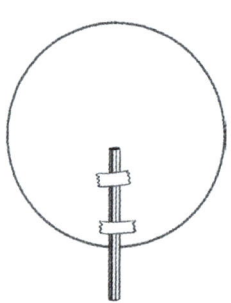
1
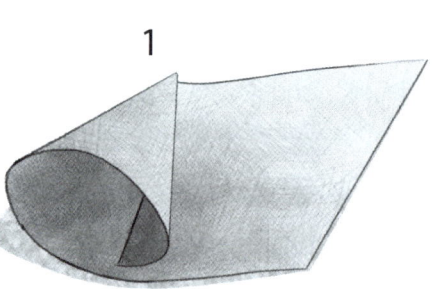

List of materials

- scissors
- card
- felt tips
- 1 sheet of white paper (for the face and tower window)
- 1 sheet of dark paper (for the tower)
- sticky tape
- drinking straw

B Complete this instruction page. First, add the list of materials. Next, draw a picture of the completed king's tower in the box. Then write clear instructions for each of the six pictures in activity A.

Instructions

List of materials

_____

_____

_____

_____

_____

1

_____

_____

_____

2

_____

_____

_____

3

_____

_____

_____

4

_____

_____

_____

_____

5

_____

_____

_____

_____

6

_____

_____

_____

_____

Storytelling

A Look at the six pictures below and write the story on the next page. Then add a title to the story.

Title: _____

_____

_____

_____

_____

_____

_____

_____

_____

_____

_____

_____

_____

_____

_____

_____

_____

_____

_____

_____

_____

_____

_____

_____

_____

_____

_____

_____

_____

_____

_____

Word fun

A Complete the ten words below and add the vowels to the definitions.

Word	Definition
ta<u>n</u>k<u>a</u>	typ<u>e</u> <u>of</u> p<u>oe</u>m
c_ _n	m_t_l p_ _c_ of m_n_y
st_ndp_p_	p_bl_c w_t_r t_p
_nc_st_r	m_mb_r _f f_m_ly fr_m l_ng _g_
h_ll_w	h_l_
m_mm_l	w_rm-bl_ _d_d _n_m_l
_ _s_s	pl_ce in d_s_rt with w_t_r
y_t_	_n_rm_ _s d_rk br_wn b_ _st
sk_l_t_n	fr_m_w_rk of b_n_s in a b_dy
v_ll_y	l_w l_nd b_tw_ _n h_lls

B Find the ten words from above in the word search.

E	V	H	R	V	A	L	L	E	Y
S	T	A	N	D	P	I	P	E	G
O	B	R	O	D	A	Y	L	O	A
C	A	H	M	A	M	M	A	L	N
O	E	S	S	F	L	R	I	D	C
I	A	H	I	T	A	N	K	A	E
N	D	U	S	S	R	O	D	O	S
E	S	N	H	O	L	L	O	W	T
M	Y	E	T	I	I	T	W	X	O
Z	S	K	E	L	E	T	O	N	R

More fun with words

A Reorder the letters and write the correct verbs. The first letter of each verb is bold.

Jumbled letters	Correct verb
adia**d**perpes	disappeared
crhne**d**	
on**a**uncne	
em**t**lub	

B Replace the words or phrases in brackets with a word from above. Remember to use the appropriate tense.

Example: The apples (~~fell~~) <u>tumbled</u> out of the basket.

1 "The play will start at five o'clock," (said) _____ the director.

2 The rain started suddenly and the audience got (wet) _____.

3 All the bad feeling (went away) _____ when the play began.

C Describe the picture below. Use words from pages 80 and 81.

_____

_____

_____

_____

_____

_____

_____

_____

Glossary

Cc
carefree having no worries

Dd
declared said firmly
defend protect against attack or loss

Ff
farewell goodbye
fond to like someone or something

Gg
glow to let off a soft, warm light

Mm
mates pairs of animals that produce young together

Oo
on behalf of expressing someone else's views

Pp
proposals ideas
proposed suggested

Rr
reject not accept something

Ss
species one type of animal or plant

Tt
tailor a person who makes clothes, especially suits
territory land that is under the control of a bird, animal or insect

200 High frequency words

A

across
after
again
air
along
am
animals
another
any
around
away

B

baby
bad
bear
because
bed
been
before

began
best
better
birds
boat
book
box
boy

C

can't
car
cat
clothes
cold
coming
couldn't
cried

D

dark
did

didn't
different
dog
door
dragon
duck

E

each
eat
eggs
end
even
ever
every
everyone
eyes

F

fast
feet
fell

find
first
fish
floppy
fly
food
found
fox
friends
fun

G

garden
gave
giant
girl
going
gone
good
gran
grandad

great
green
grow

H

hard
has
hat
head
he's
home
horse
hot
how

I

I'll
inside
its
I've

J

jumped

K

keep
key
king
know

L

last
laughed
let
let's
liked
live
lived
long
looking
looks
lots

M

_____

_____

_____

_____

_____

_____

_____

_____

_____

_____

_____

N

narrator

need

never

new

next

night

O

once

only

or

other

our

over

P

park

place

plants

play

please

pulled

Q

queen

R

rabbit

ran

really

red

right

river

room

round

run

S

_____

_____

_____

_____

_____

_____

_____

_____

T

take

tea

tell

than

that's

there's

these

thing

things

think

thought

three

through

told

took

top

_____

_____

_____

town

tree

trees

two

U

under

us

use

W

_____

_____

_____

_____

_____

_____

_____

_____

_____

_____

_____

_____

_____

_____

_____

Y

yes

A Here are all the high frequency words that begin with the letter m. Add them in the correct place to the list on page 92, putting them in alphabetical order.

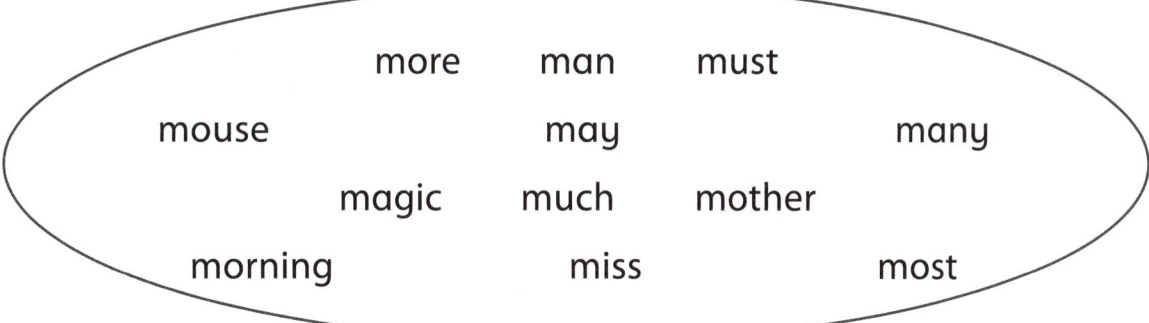

more   man   must

mouse   may   many

magic   much   mother

morning   miss   most

B Here are all the high frequency words that begin with the letter s. Add them in the correct place to the list on page 92, putting them in alphabetical order.

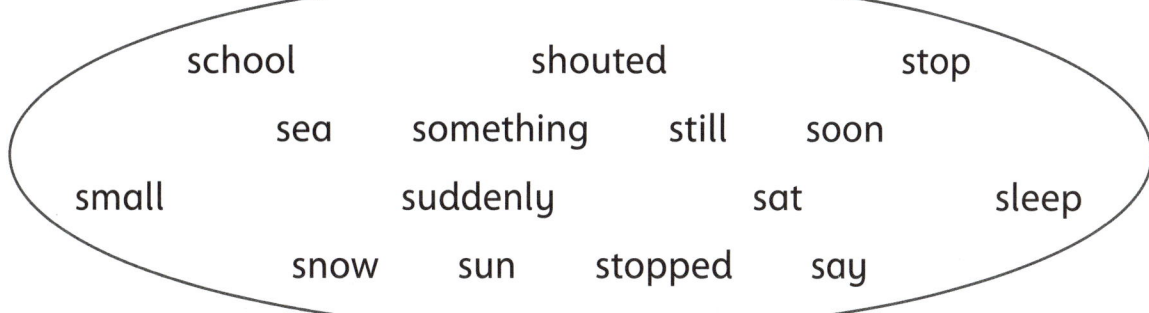

school   shouted   stop

sea   something   still   soon

small   suddenly   sat   sleep

snow   sun   stopped   say

C Here are all the high frequency words that begin with the letter w. Add them in the correct place to the list on page 92, putting them in alphabetical order.

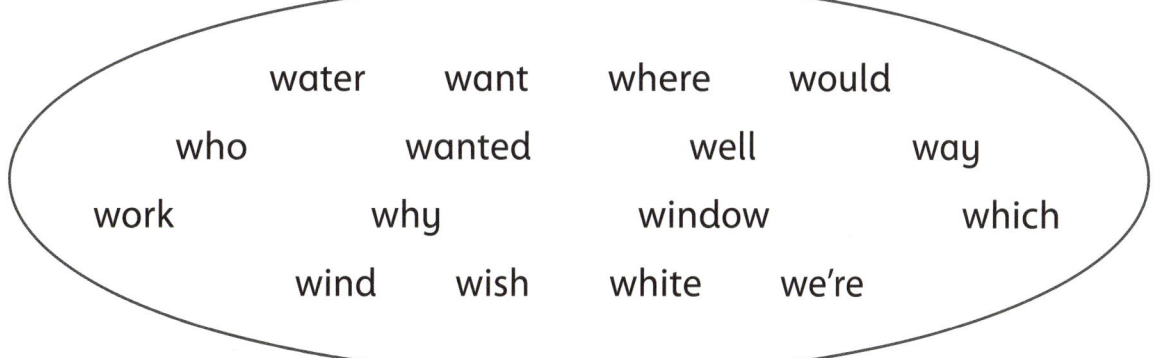

water   want   where   would

who   wanted   well   way

work   why   window   which

wind   wish   white   we're

A Find words from the list of high frequency words to put in the following boxes. Some words can go in more than one box.

nouns	adjectives	prepositions

adverbs	past verbs	present verbs

irregular verbs	question words

B In the list of high frequency words, find five words that can be used both as a noun and a verb. Make two different sentences to show the different meanings.

Example: book

He **booked** a hotel for two nights.

He enjoyed reading the adventure **book**.

_____

_____

_____

_____

_____

C Write a homophone for the following words from the high frequency list. (A homophone is a word which sounds the same but is spelled differently.)

Example: red/read

sun _____   right _____

night _____   know _____

two _____   been _____

bear _____   our _____

oar _____   hoarse _____

Key words to help you at school

These words will help you with all your subjects at school.

apparently *adverb* as it seems, so it appears

The door had apparently been locked.

apply *verb* to put something on something else

Apply a generous amount of sun cream.

apply *verb* to write a formal letter asking for a job

I am going to apply for a job as a headteacher.

apply *verb* to be relevant to someone

These rules apply to everybody.

apply *verb* to give something all your attention

You must apply yourself if you want to do well in your exams.

appropriate *adjective* suitable

Please wear suitable clothing in case the weather is bad.

argument *noun* a quarrel

I had a terrible quarrel with my sister.

argument *noun* to try to convince someone about something

He made a very good argument for going home early.

communicate *verb* to pass news or information on to other people

Nowadays, we can use the Internet to communicate.

comparison *noun* thinking about several things and how they are similar or different

In the exam, we had to do a comparison of two poems.

conclusion *noun* the ending of something

Make sure your essay has a conclusion.

conclusion *noun* a decision that you reach after a lot of thought

I came to the conclusion that I should have stayed at home.

connect *verb* to join together

You need to connect the printer to your computer.

context *noun* the words that come before or after a word or phrase which help you understand what it means

In that context I know what the word means.

continuous *adjective* going on all the time/ without a break

There was the continuous drone of traffic outside.

criteria *noun* standards or principles by which something is judged or decided

The school has a range of selection criteria for students.

describe *verb* to say what someone or something is like

How would you describe the painting? Can you describe what happened?

develop *verb* to make something or to become bigger or better

I want to develop my own singing style. Your work is developing well.

direct *adjective* as straight or quick as possible

We got on the direct train to Cairo.

direct *verb* to show someone the way

Can you direct me to the station?

effect *noun* something that happens because of something else

The music had a calming effect on us all.

effect *noun* a general impression

Fairy lights give a cosy effect.

evidence *noun* facts and information that give people reason to believe something

There was no evidence of sweets in his locker.

feedback *noun* information about how you have done on a task in order to improve

Your teacher will give you feedback on your homework.

importance *noun* the seriousness of something or the effect it has

She explained the importance of healthy eating.

indirect *adjective* not direct or straight

We took an indirect route to the station.

options *noun* one of the things that you can choose

Your options are to travel by bus or by train.

persuade *verb* to get someone to agree about something

I persuaded my mum to take us swimming.

reflect *verb* to send light or heat back from a surface

I will reflect the light back to you using this mirror.

reflect *verb* to form an image of something

The mountains were reflected in the still waters of the lake.

reflect *verb* to think seriously about something

I want you to reflect on what happened.

respond *verb* to reply or react to something or someone

I called the puppy's name, but he didn't respond.

segment *noun* a part that is cut off or can be separated from the rest of something

He ate a segment of the orange.

study *verb* to spend time learning about something

I want to study history at college.

study *verb* look at something carefully

He studied the map, looking for the house.

study *noun* the process of learning or looking at something carefully

I want to study history.

summarise *verb* to give a short statement of the main points

Can you summarise the plot in one sentence?

support *verb* to hold something so that it does not fall down

These pieces of wood support the roof.

support *verb* to give someone or something help or encouragement

I will support you.

support *verb* to encourage a sports team and want them to do well

Which football team do you support?

technique *noun* a particular method of doing something skilfully

I am playing tennis to try to improve my backhand technique.

unique *adjective* one of a kind

Your fingerprint is unique.

1 **Use these words to complete the sentences below.**

communicate   criteria

a What _____ will you use to pick the goalkeeper?

Shall we _____ by phone or text message?

comparisons   argument   develop

b I did some _____ of how many goals they had saved.

Some players _____ their skills faster than others.

I don't want to have an _____ about who I've picked.

conclusion   summarised

c I _____ my main points to give a short _____ to my speech.

direct   feedback

d The teacher's _____ praised my _____ style of speaking.

appropriate   apparently

e But _____ it's just not _____ for me to bring a pet to school.

2 **Draw a line to match each word to its synonym.**

respond   hold up

support   non-stop

develop   not straight

continuous   reply

connect   join

indirect   grow

3 **Find the following words hidden in the square.**

connect	describe	technique
criteria	develop	support
context	continuous	respond
communicate	appropriate	importance

i	c	t	i	v	e	a	p	r	a	r	a
m	f	n	c	r	i	t	e	r	i	a	p
p	r	e	o	t	d	e	v	e	l	o	p
o	i	r	n	h	m	c	m	t	c	c	r
r	s	e	n	s	t	h	l	t	y	o	o
t	u	s	e	r	i	n	t	a	x	n	p
a	p	p	c	p	o	i	i	t	e	t	r
n	p	o	t	e	s	q	c	t	i	e	i
c	o	n	t	i	n	u	o	u	s	x	a
e	r	d	y	b	a	e	u	c	r	t	t
t	t	s	h	d	e	s	c	r	i	b	e
c	o	m	m	u	n	i	c	a	t	e	y

4 Write the words in the correct box.

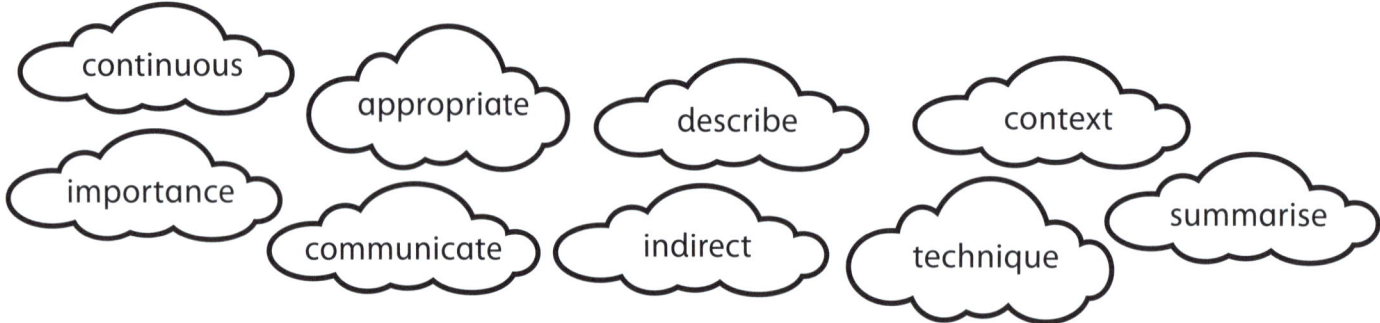

continuous

appropriate

describe

context

importance

communicate

indirect

technique

summarise

nouns	verbs	adjectives

Grammar and language terms

adjective a word that describes somebody or something
*the **blue** sky*

adverb tells you how, when, where or how something happens
now, there, slowly

adverbial phrase a group of words that acts as an adverb
*the birds flew **through the air***

alliteration occurs when two or more nearby words start with the same sound
A slow, sad, sorrowful song.

comparative the form of an adjective or adverb that expresses 'more'
faster, more peaceful

conjunction a word that joins words or phrases together
and, but, so, as

direct speech when speech marks are used to show that someone is speaking
"Can I talk to you please?" asked Sam.

homophone words that sound the same but have different meanings. They may have the same or different spellings
right, write; meat, meet

irregular verb verb that doesn't follow the same spelling pattern as regular verbs
teach, taught; am, was, will be

main clause a clause which can be used as a complete sentence
I ran

metaphor a word or phrase that describes one thing as if it were something else
The moon was a ghostly ship.

noun a person, place or thing
girl, cat, daughter, house

paragraph a group of sentences that a piece of writing is divided into. Each paragraph begins on a new line.

possessive apostrophe a punctuation mark that is used to show possession
My dog's collar. (This explains that the collar belongs to my dog.)
The boys' cards. (This explains that the cards belong to the boys.)

prefix a word or syllable joined to the front of a word to change or add to its meaning
***un**happy,* ***mis**understood*

preposition a word or phrase that tells you where or when something is in relation to something else
in, during, over, on

pronoun a word that can replace a noun
I, me, mine, myself

simile a word or phrase that compares one thing to something else
cold as ice

subordinate clause a phrase that adds information to the main clause of a sentence, but does not make sense on its own
As I walked down the road, *I saw a yellow bicycle*

suffix a word or syllable joined to the end of a word to change or add to its meaning
*point**less**, joy**ful***

superlative the form of an adjective or adverb that expresses 'most'
fastest, most peaceful

tense a verb form that shows whether events happen in the past, present or future
The Pyramids are in Egypt. (present tense)
They were built a long time ago. (past tense)
They will stand for many years to come. (future tense)
Most verbs change their spelling by adding -ed to form the past tense
walk/walked
Some have irregular spellings
catch/caught
Most verbs use 'will' to form the future tense
I will go to school tomorrow.

verb a word that shows what someone or something is doing
*The woman **raced** along the track.*